Marie Curie:
BRAVE SCIENTIST

By Joanne Mattern and Keith Brandt
Illustrated by Karen Milone

SCHOLASTIC INC.
New York   Toronto   London   Auckland   Sydney
Mexico City   New Delhi   Hong Kong   Buenos Aires

ISBN 0-439-80153-2

12 11 10 9 8 7 6 5 4 3 2 1   5 6 7 8 9 10/0

Printed in the U.S.A.

First printing, September 2005

CHAPTER 1:
"It Was So Easy!"

Little Marya Sklodowska and her big sister Bronya had discovered a wonderful game. Seven-year-old Bronya was learning to read. One day, Bronya decided to play teacher with four-year-old Marya. Bronya cut pieces of cardboard into the letters of the alphabet. She stood them against a wall and pointed at them, one by one, with a ruler. She said each letter aloud. Then she asked Marya to come up and point to each letter as Bronya said its name.

Marya got every letter of the alphabet right. Then Bronya came up with an even better game.

"Next," Bronya said, "we will study how to spell words."

Bronya could not spell very many words herself. Even so, the two little girls put together words with their cutout letters. Some of them were real words, and some of them were not. It didn't matter to the girls. The spelling game was so much fun that they played it every day for weeks.

One day Bronya was reading out loud for Mama and Papa. She read very slowly, working hard to say every word. Marya was sitting on the arm of Papa's chair. She began to fidget. At last, she sighed, stood up, and took the book out of Bronya's hands. Then she began to read out loud, easily and without a mistake.

Mr. and Mrs. Sklodowski were stunned. Bronya's face turned red with anger. She snatched the book from Marya's hands and ran from the room. Marya started to cry. "I'm sorry!" she sobbed. "I didn't do it on purpose. It's only because it was so easy!"

The four-year-old child did not understand the looks on her parents' faces. Marya thought they were angry, but they were only extremely surprised that she could read.

In the years that followed, little Marya Sklodowska would surprise many people. When she grew up, the little girl would become a famous scientist named Marie Curie. Her discoveries would change the world.

CHAPTER 2:
Learning Every Day

The Sklodowski family did not have much money. They were not famous or important. But these things did not matter to them. To the Sklodowski family of Warsaw, Poland, what *did* matter was education.

Mr. Sklodowski was a professor of mathematics and physics at a boys' school. Mrs. Sklodowska was the principal of a girls' school. (In Polish, the last names of men often end with an "i." The last names of women often end with an "a." That is why it was Mr. Sklodowski and Mrs. Sklodowska.)

The family lived at Mrs. Sklodowska's school on

Zosia Hela Manya Joseph Bronya

Freta Street. Even before the children—the three
girls, Zofia, Bronya, and Helena, and their brother,
Jozef—started school, learning was a part of their
lives. At dinner each night, they talked about
school subjects. Mama might tell about a girl who
wrote the most wonderful stories. Papa might tell
about a boy who was very good at mathematics.

They both talked about books and new ideas. And they always included their children in these talks.

This was the family into which a baby girl named Marya was born on November 7, 1867. She was a bubbly, bright-eyed little girl. Her brother and sisters fussed over her all the time. Marya was the pet of the family, and she loved the attention.

But Marya knew there was sadness in the house, too. Mrs. Sklodowska was very ill. She had tuberculosis, a disease of the lungs. In those days, the only treatment for this disease was rest. Sometimes the sick person got better. Most of the time, the patient got weaker and weaker, and eventually died. Today, tuberculosis can be cured with penicillin and other medicines. But at that time, there was little hope.

When Mrs. Sklodowska got sick, she had to stop working. The family was forced to move from their apartment. Then Mr. Sklodowski was offered an excellent job at another boys' high school. A large apartment came with this job. The family was sad to leave their old home, but they looked forward to a happy life in their new one. And everyone hoped that Mama's health would get better.

Mrs. Sklodowska was afraid that her children would catch her disease. So she did not hug or kiss them or hold any of them on her lap. The older children understood the reason for this. But Marya didn't. She only knew that hugs and kisses came from Papa and her brothers and sisters. Mama had a sweet, loving smile, and would stroke Marya's head softly. But she never kissed the child.

In many ways, big sister Zofia took Mama's place with Marya. The little girl waited for Zofia to come home from school every afternoon. Then they would go for a walk to the candy shop down the street. Zofia told stories, sang songs, and played all kinds of games with Marya. Marya was a

very bright girl. Weeks after Zofia told her a story, the little girl could repeat it exactly as she had heard it.

Marya's amazing memory worked this way all the time. She remembered every conversation she ever heard. She remembered every fact she learned. If she didn't do something she was told to do, she could not get away with saying, "Oh, I forgot."

Marya's parents were very pleased that she was so bright. But they felt there was time enough for studying when Marya went to school. Now, the little girl should run and play.

And Marya liked to play, especially with the wooden blocks their uncle had given them for Christmas. "Here," he said. "Now you can build castles and houses and bridges."

At first, the children used the blocks that way. Then they found a better game to play. War! Jozef and Helena were one team. Bronya and Marya were the other. Each team would build a fort and

open fire. Blocks would fly back and forth across the playroom, until both forts were knocked down. Marya remembered those wild battles for the rest of her life.

She also remembered many wonderful vacations in the country. Every summer, the family went

to visit relatives in the countryside. Marya loved running barefoot through the grassy fields, climbing trees, wading in the streams, and eating cherries and apples she picked herself.

For many people, however, life in Poland was not happy. The country was not free. Russia ruled Poland. Polish schoolchildren had to learn their lessons in Russian. They were forbidden to speak their own language in school.

When the Russians said Polish children should not be taught much science, Mr. Sklodowski was sad. He took his scientific equipment—scales, minerals, and test tubes—and put them in a glass case in his study.

Marya liked to look in the glass case. She thought the shelves held the most beautiful things she had ever seen. "Papa, what do you call these pretty, shiny things?" she asked one day.

"That is phy-sics ap-pa-ra-tus," he answered.

The words sounded lovely to Marya's ears. *Some day*, she thought to herself, *I will have phy-sics ap-pa-ra-tus of my own.* Of course, the five-year-old did not know what the words "physics apparatus" meant. She only knew she wouldn't rest until she understood everything about them.

CHAPTER 3:
Sad Days

Marya had glorious dreams for the future. But right now, the family had many problems. In September of 1873, when Marya was almost six years old, Mr. Sklodowski received bad news from the school principal. Mr. Sklodowski's job was being made less important, and his salary was being cut. The family was ordered to move out of their apartment at the school.

The seven Sklodowskis moved to a smaller apartment. Even then, there wasn't enough money for their needs. So the family took in ten of Mr. Sklodowski's students to board with them.

The bedrooms were filled with boarders, and the Sklodowski children slept on couches and cots in the dining room. The children had to be up early every morning to put away the bedding and set the table for breakfast. There was no privacy, and the best food had to go to the people who paid the rent.

To make matters worse, Mrs. Sklodowska's health was failing. The doctor said she must go to a warm, sunny place for a long rest. Even though it meant using the last of the family's savings, Mrs. Sklodowska and Zofia went to the south of France.

They came home a year later. Marya rushed to welcome them. Maybe Mama would finally be well enough to scoop up her little girl and kiss her for the very first time! But Mrs. Sklodowska was thin and very weak. She was even sicker than when she had left for France.

In January of 1876, when Marya was eight years old, one of the boarders fell ill with typhus, a very serious disease. Bronya and Zofia caught it from him. After weeks of very high fever, Bronya began to

recover. But fourteen-year-old Zofia died. It came as a terrible blow to Marya. Zofia had been like a mother to her.

The sadness did not end with Zofia's death. Mrs. Sklodowska's tuberculosis was growing worse. Finally, on May 9, 1878, she died, too.

Every time Marya thought of Mama and Zofia, she felt lonely. The only way she could escape from her sorrow was to bury herself in books. Marya read everything she could get her hands on—poetry, textbooks, novels, and scientific journals from her father's library. She read books written in Polish, Russian, French, and German. And she remembered every word she read. The harder the book was, the more she liked it. Studying took her away from the sadness in her life and opened up a whole new world.

CHAPTER 4:
School Days

Marya's brother and sisters sometimes teased her for studying all the time. They found one thing about Marya especially funny. Marya could shut out all the sounds around her when she was reading. People would talk to her, even call her name, but she heard nothing. All the Sklodowski children and the many boarders studied at the dining-room table at the same time. So there was always a lot of noise. But Marya sat in her chair and read on, floating in a sea of silence.

One day, the children came up with an idea. They put a chair on each side of Marya's. Then they put another chair behind her. Next, they stacked two more chairs on top of the first three. Finally, they laid a chair on top of all of them. Marya was surrounded by a pyramid of six chairs.

Through all the giggling and building, Marya kept on reading. For half an hour, the children watched and waited. At last, Marya closed her book and started to get up.

As she pushed back her chair, the pyramid came crashing down. Chairs tumbled left and right. The mischief makers howled with laughter.

Marya didn't laugh—she was startled. She stood still for a moment, watching Helena and Bronya rolling on the floor, giggling wildly. Then Marya angrily picked up her book and walked out of the room.

Even though she didn't find it funny at the time, Marya never forgot the pyramid of chairs. Years later, the ability to keep her mind locked on what she was doing helped her to become one of the world's greatest scientists. Sometimes coworkers in her laboratory complained when they could not get her attention. Then she would laugh and tell them the joke of the "pyramid of chairs."

As a child, Marya's love of reading and her great memory made her a prize pupil. At Mademoiselle Sikorska's school for girls, as at all Polish schools, classes were supposed to be taught in Russian. But the Poles refused to give up their own language. They held secret classes in Polish history, which were taught in Polish. Of course, they could not let the Russian school inspectors know what they were doing.

There was a special bell signal to let everyone know when an inspector entered Marya's school. When this signal sounded, the Polish books disappeared. Any time the inspector came into Marya's classroom, the teacher called on her to recite.

Marya stood straight, her face calm and serious. Her hair was neatly braided and tied with a dark ribbon. She wore the school uniform: a navy blue wool dress with steel buttons and a starched white collar. On her feet were dark stockings and polished, black, high-laced shoes.

Using her faultless memory and speaking
perfect Russian, Marya repeated page after page of
the Russian history book. She always pleased the
inspector. But she hated everything about his visit.
She loved her country and her language. It was
painful for her to make believe that she was a
faithful subject of the Russian rulers. When the
inspector was gone, she cried. Not even the praise
of her classmates could take away the shame she
felt at having to play this terrible game.

Marya graduated from Mademoiselle
Sikorska's school at the top of her class. Then
she entered the best girls' high school in
Warsaw. Marya plunged into her studies.
Math and science were her favorite subjects, but
she did well in everything. Every year she won top
honors. When she graduated, on June 12,
1883, the fifteen-year-old girl was awarded
a gold medal. It was the highest prize a student
could get.

Now, Marya wanted to go to college. There, she could really explore the world of science. But women were not allowed to go to college in Poland. Marya was furious. It was like being told to lock her mind in a small room and keep it there forever.

Marya lost all interest in everything around her. She didn't want to eat. She sat staring out a window for hours. She cried when her family tried to cheer her up. At last, her father

sent her to stay with relatives in the country.
He hoped that the rest would lift her out of her
gloom.

At first, it didn't seem to help. But, at last,
the fun and beauty of country living began to
work on Marya. As she wrote to her best friend
Kazia, "There is plenty of water for swimming
and boating, which delights me. I am learning
to row—I am getting on quite well—and the
bathing is ideal. We do everything that comes

into our heads. We sleep sometimes at night and sometimes by day. We dance, and we do so many crazy things that sometimes we deserve to be locked up!"

When Marya returned to her home in Warsaw, she felt a lot better. She also had a plan for her future.

CHAPTER 5:
Secret Studies

Marya knew she had to go to college. She decided to work and save her money. Then, when she had enough, she would go to France and study science at the Sorbonne University.

During the day, Marya gave lessons to young children. At night, she attended the "floating university." This was a group of people who met in secret. Some were women who were not allowed to go to college. Some were men who could not afford to go to college. The teachers were Polish patriots who did not want their people to be ignorant.

At the floating university, Marya studied anatomy, natural history, chemistry, biology, mathematics, and literature. She also found time to teach literature and Polish history to working women. This was the only way these women would ever get any education.

When Marya turned eighteen, she was still a long way from her goal. Then she and Bronya thought up a new plan. Bronya also wanted to go to college. She wanted to become a doctor. The sisters decided that Bronya would take their savings and begin studying at the Sorbonne in Paris. Marya would get a job as a governess and send her earnings to Bronya. When Bronya became a doctor, she would bring Marya to Paris and pay *her* way through school.

For the next six years, Marya worked as a governess for a family with two children. She did not like her job, but she knew it would give her and Bronya brighter futures.

Meanwhile, her sister finished medical school.

Finally, in 1891, Bronya sent for Marya. On November 3, 1891, Marya enrolled at the Sorbonne, as Marie Sklodowska. It was the first step on a path that would lead to greatness.

CHAPTER 6:
Marie and Pierre

At first, Marya lived with Bronya and her husband. But her sister's home was noisy. Marya wanted to be alone so she could study all the time. So she moved into a small, bare room in an attic near the school. Marya spent next to nothing on rent and food. Almost all of her money went to school and books. Every moment was spent studying or attending classes.

Marie's life was far from easy. The classes were taught in French, which was a difficult language for her. Also, her French classmates were way ahead of her in their scientific education.

But Marie's heart and mind were set on one goal—a life dedicated to science. No obstacle was too great for her to overcome. Sure enough, in 1893, she received an advanced degree in physics—and was first in her class! One year later, Marie received an advanced degree in mathematics. This time she was second in her class.

Marie's education still wasn't finished. She continued to study at the Sorbonne and to do laboratory research. Not long before this, scientists had discovered that an element called uranium gave off unexplained rays. We now know that these rays are atomic radiation. But it was a total mystery in the 1890s. Marie set out to solve the mystery of uranium.

About this time, Marie met Pierre Curie, a professor of physics at the Sorbonne. Their interest in science brought them together, and their friendship soon turned to love. They were married on July 26, 1895. Marie and Pierre had two children, Irene and Eve. They were a happy family. Marie and Pierre were also partners in science. With her husband's help and advice, Marie Curie continued her research in radioactivity.

CHAPTER 7:

Triumphs and Dangers

In 1898, Marie and Pierre discovered two elements. Marie named one polonium after her homeland, Poland. They named the other element radium. For this great work, the Curies were awarded the Nobel Prize for Physics in 1903. Marie Curie was the first woman to receive the Nobel Prize.

Then, in 1906, tragedy again came into Marie's life. Pierre was walking down the street. As usual, he was thinking hard. Pierre did not pay attention to where he was going. He stepped off a curb, right into the path of a horse-drawn wagon. The wagon hit Pierre and killed him.

Once again, Marie coped with sorrow by burying herself in work. She also devoted herself to raising Irene and Eve.

Marie continued to work with radium until she finally found a way to make it pure. This form of radium was—and still is—used to treat cancer patients. For this work, Marie Curie was awarded the Nobel Prize for Chemistry in 1911. It was the first time anyone had ever won two Nobel Prizes!

Working with radioactive elements was bad for Marie's health. Today we know that radiation is very dangerous. People who work with radioactive materials must wear special clothes to protect themselves. But in the early days, no one knew that radiation was dangerous. Marie handled radioactive materials with her bare hands. She often had serious burns on her fingers. Marie also suffered from terrible pains in her joints. She was tired all the time. Today, we know these are symptoms of radiation sickness. But Marie just thought she was sick because she worked so hard.

Though she became world famous, Marie Curie wanted to be nothing more than a scientist and mother. She worked in her laboratory until she died on July 4, 1934.

Marie once said, "Nothing in life is to be feared. It is only to be understood." Marie did not care about glory or money. Only science, and what it could do for people, were truly important to the great Madame Curie. The little girl who had seen such beauty in her father's "phy-sics ap-pa-ra-tus" had grown into one of the world's greatest scientists.